A story to introduce 'A Night On Bare Mountain' by Modest Mussorgsky

THE CRAZY ALIEN BALL

GW01005466

To Hannah Love

Editor: Robin Norman
Illustrations: David John Souster
Design and Layout: John Good Holbrook
Cd recording issued under license from Sanctuary Records Group Ltd.

IMP
International
MUSIC
Publications

© International Music Publications Limited Griffin House 161 Hammersmith Road London W6 8BS England
Published 2004

Introducing Classical Music Through Stories
A Triple Resource
MUSIC • LITERACY • ART

As a specialist art teacher I found there were so many possibilities to explore an aspect of art such as colour in an unusual approach, and the project based on Crazy Alien Ball fitted very neatly into the art curriculum.

I decided not to show the children the illustrations at first, but asked them to build pictures in their minds. They were full of exciting ideas and were totally absorbed in their pictures as the music played in a loop after the initial story reading.

I was so inspired by this I have decided to do a lengthier project with next year's Year 4, introducing an IT element. Scanning in images and experimenting with colour techniques would be a valuable progression, as would using lettering programmes to work with the illustrations. Another interesting development could be the creation of a class collage using cut out images assembled against an atmospheric background. Wonderful!

Jan Fleming, Specialist Art Teacher, Somerhill, Tonbridge

The Year 3 class were enchanted by the combination of music, text and illustrations in William the Crack Shot Kid, and were very quickly involved in the written task I set them. They loved writing their own versions of the story to fit the music and I was particularly impressed by the inspired work produced by children with learning difficulties. Ideas came, sentences flowed and stories evolved, and the oil pastel illustrations the children did were an added bonus. The activity extended to a whole day and the session finished with the class reading each other their stories as the music was played yet again, followed by requests to do the same task the next day!

Ann Bourne, Year 3 Generalist Teacher, Bedgebury Junior School

---

THE 6 TITLES OF STORIES IN THE SERIES, AND THE MUSIC ON WHICH THEY ARE BASED

Set One

WASP ALERT IN MINIBUG BONANZALAND
Overture:The Wasps
by Ralph Vaughan Williams
British
1872 - 1958

THE INCREDIBLE SPINNING WHEEL
Omphale's Spinning Wheel
by Camille Saint-Saëns
French
1835 - 1921

———————●———————

Set Two

WILLIAM THE CRACK SHOT KID
Overture: William Tell
by Gioacchino Rossini
Italian
1792 - 1868

THE CRAZY ALIEN BALL
A Night on Bare Mountain
by Modest Mussorgsky
Russian
1839 - 1881

———————●———————

Set Three

BILLY BRIGGS, BIG ON SKATES
The Moldau from 'Ma Vlast'
by Frederick Smetana
Czech
1824 - 1884

JUPITER COVE
Jupiter from 'The Planets Suite'
by Gustav Holst
British
1874 - 1934

———————●———————

ABOUT THE BOOK

The books are designed to be used as part of your scheme of work for music, literacy and art and will particularly help generalists, as they are straight forward, interesting and fun to use.

If you ask children what they think of classical music they often say 'It's boring.' That's an understandable reaction. Classical music doesn't have the 'immediacy' of pop, rock, rap etc. It lacks a constant even beat, often lacks lyrics and is usually longer than the average pop song.

However pieces such as *The Sorcerer's Apprentice* usually prove very popular with young children. Why? Because they have strong contrasting dynamics, are very descriptive, and best of all, they have a story. It is the story, particularly when combined with illustrations, that is the instant attraction.

Many pieces of classical music either do not have a story at all, or have an inappropriate one – too old, too complicated, too scary or simply too uninteresting. This series uses original stories written specifically for young children and inspired by short interesting pieces of music from a variety of different cultures. Although the stories are original, they bear some association with the title and flavour of the music.

HOW TO USE THIS BOOK

1. AS A MUSIC RESOURCE

Simply read the story to the class, showing the pictures on the way, with the music playing at the same time. It tells you in the story when to put on the CD. Make sure you play the music loudly enough for it to be clearly heard, but not so loud that it overpowers your voice. It is a good idea to have the remote control on hand so you can adjust the volume control when necessary! Tell the children beforehand that you want them to be silent throughout the story.

You need to read the story so it 'matches' the music. For this reason, time indications (e.g. 3:42) have been included on the page and you will need to keep an eye on the counter of the CD player, in order to pace your reading of each section of text. The story has been flexibly designed to enhance the piece of music. This means that sometimes the children will simply be listening to the music, while looking at the illustration which you are holding up. Their imaginations will be working away, because they are in effect 'suspended' within the story. Try it out beforehand so you have a feel for how the story fits the music. Remember the story is only the vehicle for capturing the children's attention. It is important that it doesn't dominate to such an extent that the music becomes lost in the background, secondary to the story.

After listening you might like to talk about the contrasts in the music. For example loud/quiet, fast/slow, high/low and smooth/bouncy. Discuss the feelings the music evoked; such as fear, calm, wonder or amazement. In your discussion, use descriptive words – scary, peaceful, gentle, mysterious, tense, magical. All this is valuable work, focusing the children on the style, mood and atmosphere of the music.

The next stage is to play the music *without* reading the story. Just show the pictures, pausing for as long as you feel on each illustration so they can mentally follow the story through the pictures.

And finally listen to the music without any verbal or visual aids at all. Now the children's imaginations are 'buzzing' they will enjoy the music in its own right a great deal more than they would have done, had they heard it without the benefit of the story the first time round.

2. AS A LITERACY RESOURCE

It is usual for creative writing to be inspired by a story, a picture, an illustration, an experience or a poem. With this resource the music adds a further starting point, as well as an additional dimension to the story. There are three ways in which to use the resource:-
1) Read the story without the music, showing the pictures, and get the children to evolve their own stories based on the same characters.
2) Use the music only, as a brainstorming exercise for the whole class, to inspire poetry or a piece of creative writing.
3) Use the story in conjunction with the music (see 'HOW TO USE THE BOOK AS A MUSIC RESOURCE') to show how the two media interact. This might stimulate poetry or a piece of creative/imaginative writing.

3. AS AN ART RESOURCE

This resource can be used in three distinctive ways, either individually or worked together to form a project of half a term or a term's duration.

The first stage is to give children the opportunity to look at the work of illustrative artists, analysing the media and examining the various techniques used, as well as considering how the text and illustration are incorporated on the page. This is an important part of the art design section of the National Curriculum.

The second stage is for the children to engage with the music and the story, absorbing the atmospheres and moods evoked by the storyline, then to develop their own ideas using materials related to illustrations they have seen.

The final stage is to use I.T. If facilities permit, the children should learn how to scan their pictures into *Publisher*, and then to apply text to the page so that the best possible layout is achieved.

About 'A Night on Bare Mountain'

Modest Petrovich Mussorgsky lived from 1839 to 1881 and was one of the so-called 'mighty-five' composers who came together in St. Petersburg in the 1860's to create music with a truly Russian voice which would speak in loud contrast to the European popular styles of the day. The others in the 'mighty five' were Borodin, Cui, Balakirev and Rimsky-Korsakov, but Mussorgsky is considered the most radical. Many of his works were unfinished, and their editing and posthumous publication were mainly carried out by Rimsky-Korsakov.

'A Night on Bare Mountain', sometimes called Night on Bald Mountain, was written in 1867 and originally entitled *Saint John's Night on the Bare Mountain*. It was inspired by a scene of a witches' sabbath. Mussorgsky produced two other versions of the piece and it is the third version, a choral introduction for Act 3 of Sorochintsy Fair (1873) that Rimsky-Korsakov re-worked into the piece as we now know it. The spine-tingling music depicts all sorts of demons and spirits of darkness, devils and hobgoblins having a party on a dark and desolate mountain. Towards the end of the piece we hear the church bells heralding dawn to represent the fleeing of the evil spirits.

Now enjoy the story!

As Harry climbed Bare Mountain he kept
recalling what everyone had said.
"You hear terrible stories about the Mountain, Harry!
Balls of light dropping out of the sky... Aliens... All sorts!"
Harry chuckled to himself.
He hadn't come across any aliens so far.
And now he was right at the top
the view was breathtaking.
Although... the sky *was* beginning to darken...

CD ON

0.07

And what was that awful noise like an electric saw whining in the distance?

0.15

Harry watched in horror as sweeps and swathes of darkness wrapped themselves around and around the mountain, and the whining grew and grew... Until suddenly, incredibly, it stopped.

0.40

In no time at all, though, it was back again and Harry felt relieved
that he'd got his sleeping bag with him. He snuggled down to the bottom
and did the zip right up to the top. Then he blocked his ears.
But it couldn't block out the terrible noise. Nor the blackening
sky that curled itself around Harry's sleeping bag.

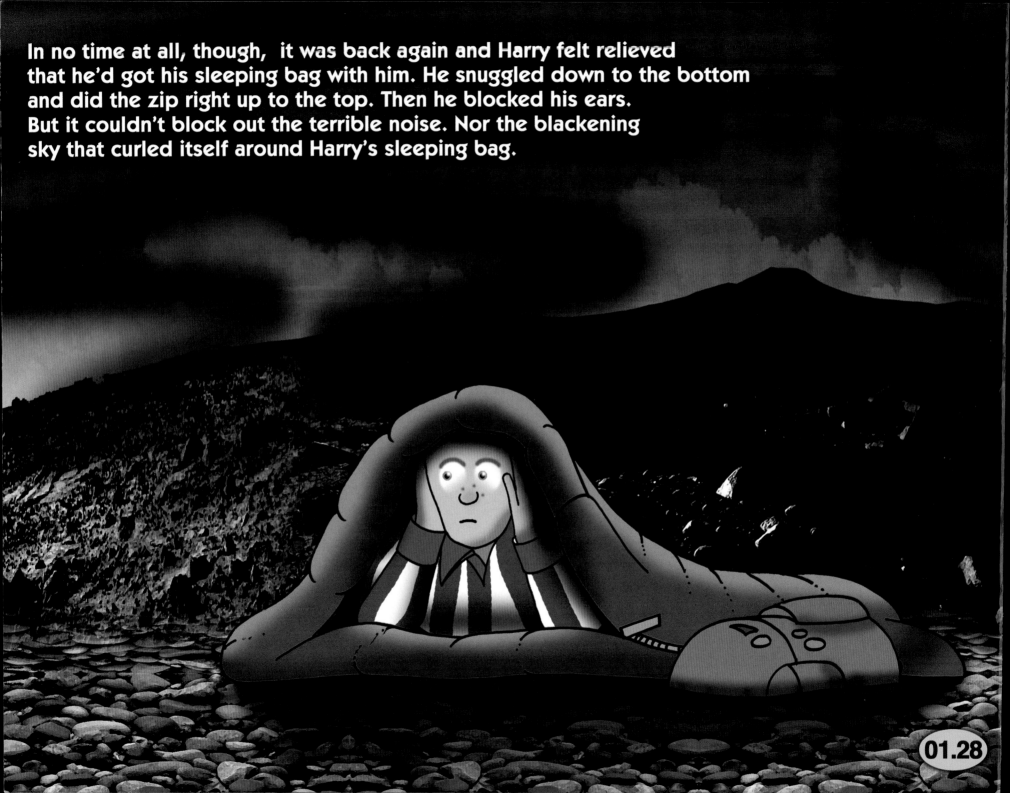

01.28

"That's better," Harry said to himself a few moments later.
I'll take a peep now. Just a little peep."
Cautiously he poked his head out of his sleeping bag and looked round.

01.44

An awful smell hung over the mountain.
It sent Harry diving straight back under cover.

02.04

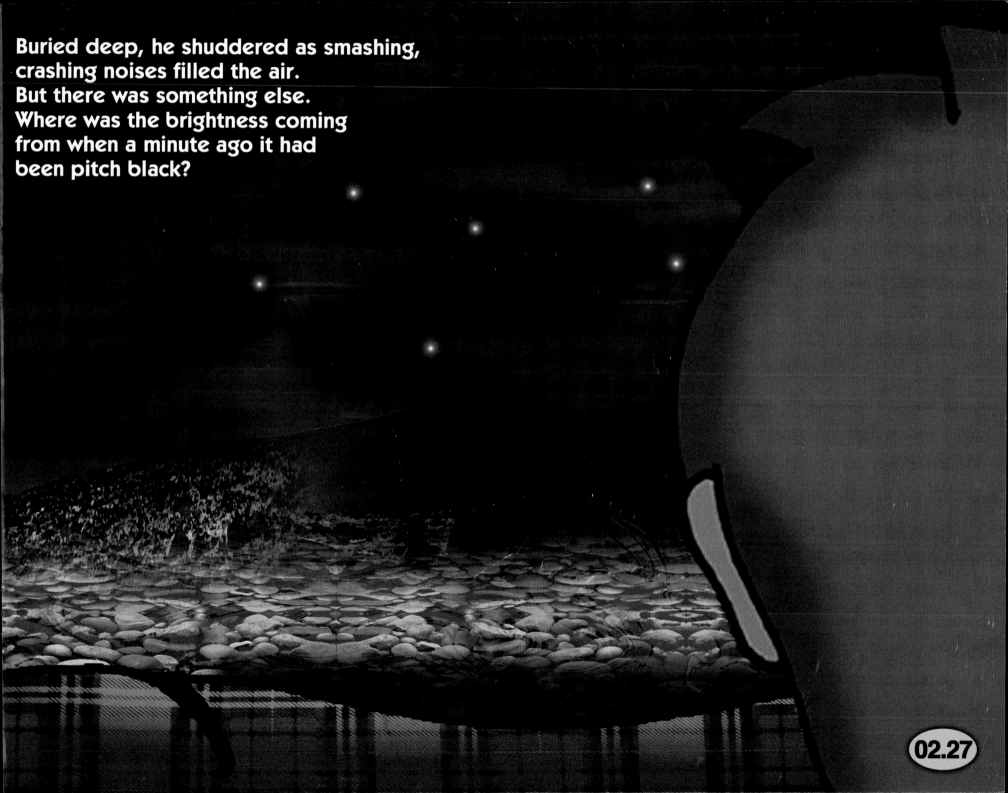

Buried deep, he shuddered as smashing,
crashing noises filled the air.
But there was something else.
Where was the brightness coming
from when a minute ago it had
been pitch black?

02.27

Heart beating wildly, he took another look.
And what a sight it was.
Hundreds of bubbles of light lit up the sky.
Harry gasped. They were drifting towards
the mountain. "Oh no!" he whispered.
"Whatever's going on?"

03.04

"A *Ball* is what's going on!"
Harry nearly jumped out of his skin at the
sound of the high pitched raspy voice.
One of the bubbles had alighted right
next to him on the mountain top.
A small wrinkled creature was climbing
out of its bubble capsule.
Harry stayed perfectly still and silent while
the creature eyed him suspiciously.

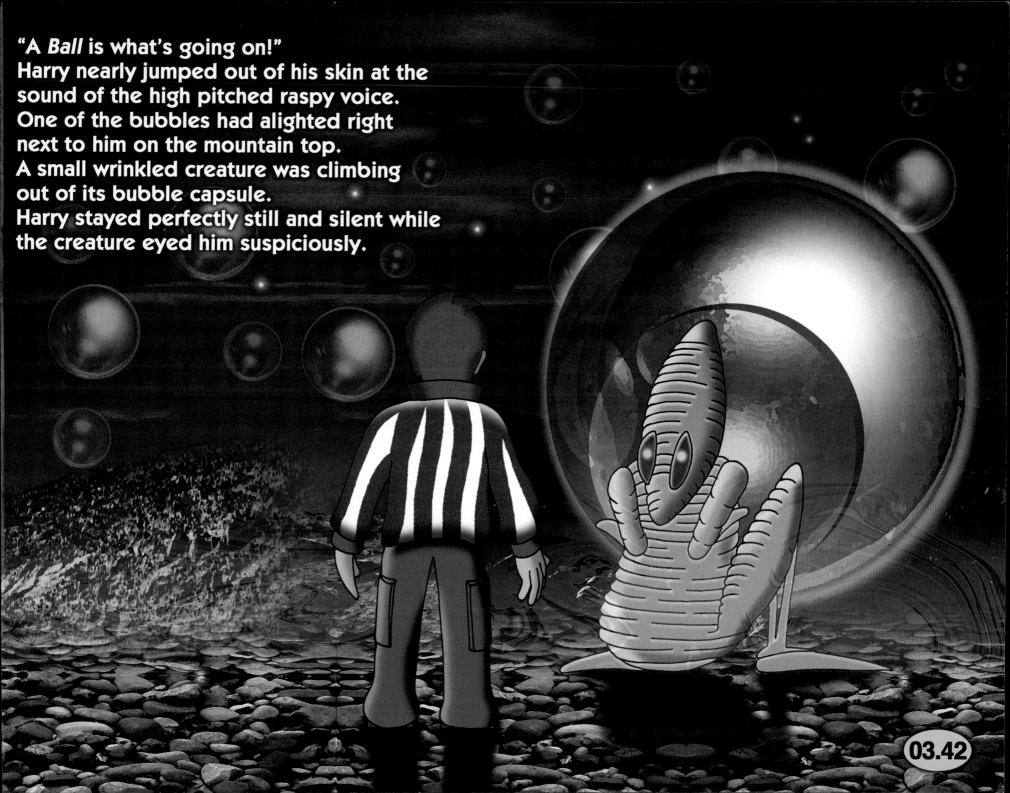

03.42

"Who are you?" it asked eventually.
"Er... my name's... Harry."
"Where's your capsule, *Harry?*"
"Ju- just over there..."
"Hmmm...." said the creature.
Then it jumped off like a massive grass hopper.
Harry shivered and peered down the mountain side.
It looked slippery and black.

04.27

Up in the sky the rest of the bubbles
seemed to be growing bigger.
No wonder. They were coming closer.
Harry's eyes widened.

04.50

Then he gasped. On every part of the mountain bubbles were landing, and all sorts of weird and revolting creatures were climbing out of the massive capsules.

05.25

"Mustn't let them see me," muttered Harry as he scrambled into a crevice in the rocks, dragging his sleeping bag and his rucksack after him.
And there he sat, trembling and fearful, while the party thundered on around him.

05.59

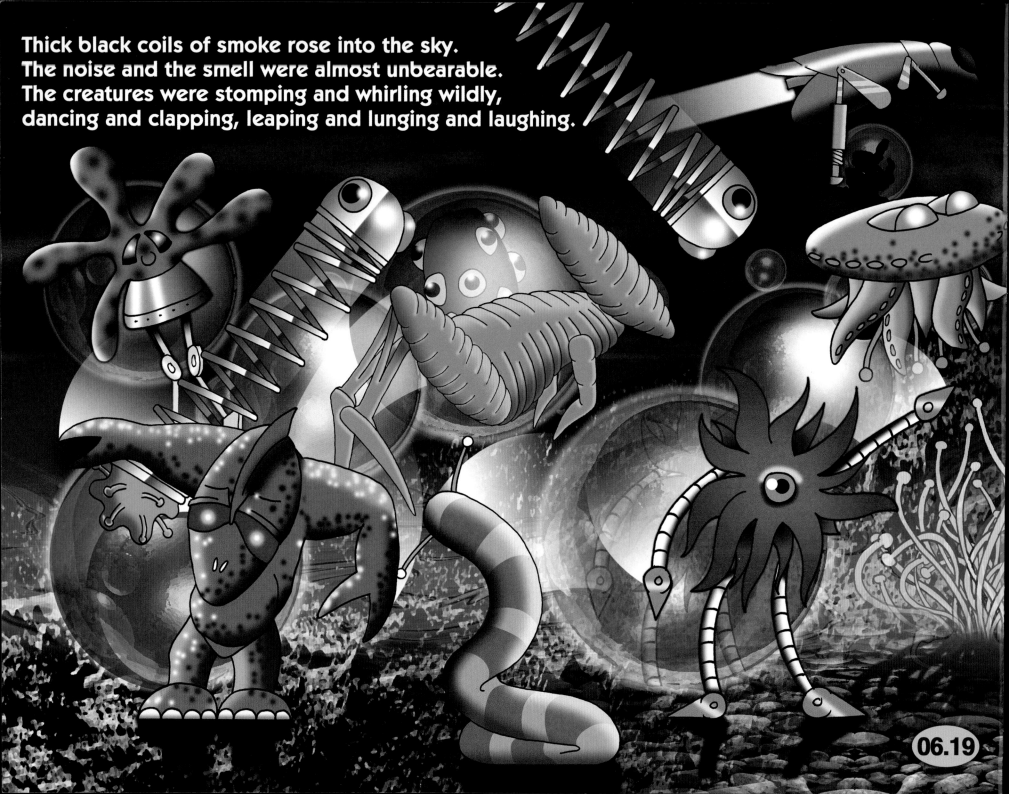

It was just when Harry thought he'd go mad if he had to
put up with another second of this alien party,
that the noise suddenly fizzled away.
And the beautiful sound of bells filled the air.

07.27

Harry waited until he was sure it was safe, then crept out of his hiding place.
The creatures were no more than flaking gossamer in the distance.
"They're afraid of daylight," said Harry to himself.
"When they heard the morning bells they fled in fear."

08.03

He looked up. Sunlight was threading its way round the peaks of the mountain.

08.15

The fields below were spread out like a patchwork quilt.
It was a beautiful day.

08.33

Harry pulled his sleeping bag out of the crevice and put it in his rucksack. Then he stood up straight and stretched.

08.47

The sky was silver blue and the sun's rays trickled down the side of the mountain. It was an amazing sight.

09.13

Little drops of sun spread over the fields and turned the green grasses to pink and red, mauve and violet, rose and indigo.

09.46

Harry slowly began to make his way down the mountain, wondering if he could possibly have imagined the crazy alien ball.

10.04

By the time he'd reached the bottom he was quite certain the whole thing had simply been a bad dream.

He never noticed the fold of thin bubble skin caught up on a patch of prickly gorse right at the foot of Bare Mountain.

End

Also Available from IMP, these Great Schemes of Work for Specialist and Non-Specialist Teachers

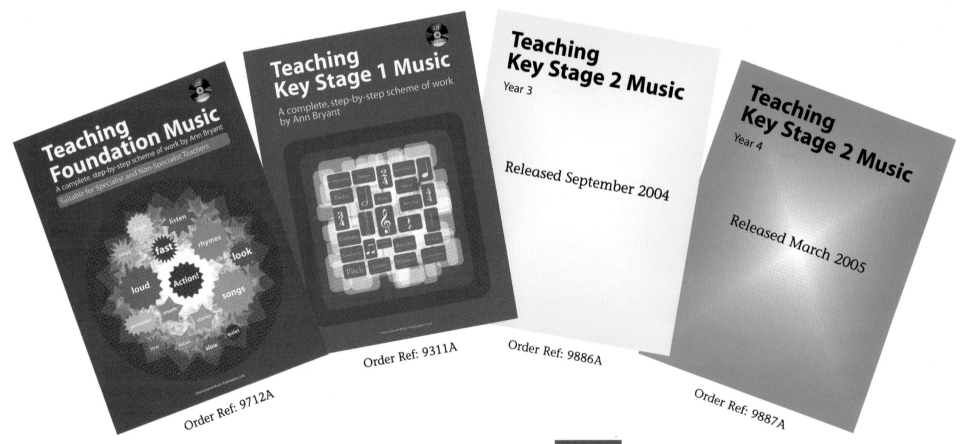

Teaching Foundation Music
A complete, step-by-step scheme of work by Ann Bryant
Suitable for Specialist and Non-Specialist Teachers

Order Ref: 9712A

Teaching Key Stage 1 Music
A complete, step-by-step scheme of work by Ann Bryant

Order Ref: 9311A

Teaching Key Stage 2 Music
Year 3
Released September 2004

Order Ref: 9886A

Teaching Key Stage 2 Music
Year 4
Released March 2005

Order Ref: 9887A

IMP, for all your Music at School needs.
www.music-at-school.co.uk

IMP
International MUSIC Publications

International Music Publications Ltd.
Griffin House, 161 Hammersmith Road, London, W6 8BS